Companion Workbook

For

The One Thing:

The Surprisingly Simple Truth Behind

Extraordinary Results

By

Gary Keller with Jay Papasan

Book Nerd

Table of Contents

Note to readers:
This is an unofficial companion workbook of Papasan's and Keller's The One Thing. This workbook is designed to enrich your reading experience and help you put the principles into action. Buy the original book here: https://www.amazon.com/ONE-Thing-Surprisingly-Extraordinary-Results/dp/1885167776

Chapter One of The One Thing

In your opinion, do you accomplish a lot on any given day?

What matters most to you? Keller and Papasan say that all things don't matter equally and that it's best to go small.

What is your specific focus? It's best to have a narrow focus and go small for the one goal you have in life at this point.

Chapter Two of The One Thing

What is the one thing you want to focus on?

Have you ever recreated the domino effect in your life? What are some things you have set into motion that led to big outcomes? These can be positive or negative things. The domino effect produced big results because it's sequential and one step leads to the next. The steps have to be taken in order.

Chapter Three of The One Thing

Who has influenced you in life or helped you get to the next stage of life?

What's the one thing you are passionate about in life?

What's your strongest skill?

What's the one way you want to impact society, your community, or your cause?

Lies Surrounding the One Thing

Not all things are a priority nor matter to the same degree. What is your top priority?

The second lie is that multitasking is effective. Have you ever multitasked? How did that work out for you?

Do you consider yourself to be disciplined?

Do you believe that you have strong willpower and that you can summon your willpower any time you want?

Do you feel that your life is balanced? Is it possible to have a balanced life?

Do you believe that having a big life and big goals is a good thing?

Chapter Four of The One Thing

Do you often find yourself being busy yet unproductive?

Instead of creating a to-do list, create a must-do list. What's on your list?

How will you apply the 80/20 principle, also known as Pareto's principle to your life? First, find the twenty percent that will give you the biggest results, and then find twenty percent of that amount.

Chapter Five of The One Thing

Multitasking has been proven to be ineffective. How can you avoid multitasking and keep focusing on just one thing? Do you feel stressed out when you multitask?

Do you ever talk on the phone while doing other tasks like surfing the web or driving?

| |
| |
| |

Chapter Six of The One Thing

Discipline isn't required for success; it's usually only used as a catalyst. One should rely on habits to create natural discipline. What are some of your current habits? Which habits would you like to adapt? Forming a new habit is harder than maintaining it, and some discipline may be required when forming a new habit. The authors of *The One Thing* say it's important to form one habit at a time.

Chapter Seven of The One Thing

Willpower can't be called upon at any time, and it's a limited resource. It's also unpredictable and needs to be replenished from time to time. Don't do your most important work while your willpower is low. What will you use your willpower for?

Chapter Eight of The One Thing

Life is often unbalanced. When one strives to reach a big goal, life becomes unbalanced and that's normal. The authors point out that amazing accomplishments happen at the extremes, not when everything is balanced. Have you ever felt off balance? Was it worth it? Did you accomplish your goals?

Have you ever gambled with your time by deferring something? Were you ever able to get to do what you wanted or did life pass you by?

| |
| |
| |
| |

The authors suggest counterbalancing one's life when things get unbalanced. They don't recommend being unbalanced in one's personal life for a long time, but when it comes to work, that's ok. Personal life should be tightly counterbalanced. How will you counterbalance your life?

| |
| |
| |
| |
| |
| |
| |
| |
| |
| |

It's normal for life to become unbalanced when one focuses on one's priority. Instead of balancing, it's best to prioritize. Keep in mind that the longer you focus on your priority, the less balanced your life will feel. How much time will you spend on your priority?

| |
| |
| |

Chapter Nine of The One Thing

How often do you think big? Have you played small in the past?

How can you change your thinking so you can change your results?

How often do you think outside the box?

Have you ever take big action that may have been intimidating but you knew it was necessary to move your life forward? What other big actions do you plan on taking?

Are you afraid of failure? How can you take action in spite of your fear? Move past your fear and take the right action anyway. Don't be afraid to fail because failure will help you succeed in the long run.

How often do you study successful people? It's a good idea to learn from those who have accomplished what you want to accomplish.

Chapter Ten of The One Thing

Do you find yourself asking the right questions? If you get your problems resolved, then you are likely asking yourself and others the right questions.

The authors encourage you to ask the **Focusing Question** to come up with the right answers: what one thing can you do that will make everything simpler or unnecessary?

Whenever you're reached a big goal in life, do you think this happened by accident or because you worked to reach this goal?

Expand your perspective to discover your one thing. Your one thing will help you find your purpose in life and will allow you to create a vision for your life. How will you expand your perspective? Where do you think you're headed in life at this point?

What is your one thing right now?

Chapter Eleven of The One Thing

Are you having a hard time breaking a bad habit?

Do you believe that focusing on the one thing will change your life? The authors say that you must believe that it will help you for it to be effective in your life.

Are you feeling lost in life? If you are, the authors suggest asking yourself the focusing question.

How long has it taken you to form a new habit? The authors say that the average time that it takes for someone to develop a new habit is sixty-six days.

| |
| |
| |
| |

How will you remind yourself to work on your habit? What reminders will you set?

| |
| |
| |
| |
| |
| |
| |
| |
| |
| |

Are you part of a support group? Keller and Papasan recommend joining one to help you reach your goals.

| |
| |
| |
| |
| |

Chapter Twelve of The One Thing

What is one small and specific question you can ask to get the answer you're looking for? It's best to ask small and specific question to address the issue.

When you got an answer to your question, was it a doable answer, a "stretch, answer", or a far off answer? These are the three types of answers one can get according to Papasan and Keller. The "stretch" answers are hard to put into practice because the practice isn't always within your reach.

How can you focus on big goals rather than just doable goals?

Who do you follow? Which role model would you like to meet?

What are the trends and benchmarks of your chosen goal or path?

Chapter Thirteen of The One Thing

Have you ever changed your priorities and perspective?

| |
| |
| |
| |
| |
| |
| |
| |
| |
| |

Do you value happiness and understand how to obtain it continuously? The authors tell a story about a beggar with a bottomless begging bowl. It's important that your purpose doesn't become a bottomless bowl. Take the time to enjoy your life.

| |
| |
| |
| |
| |
| |
| |

What is your grand vision for your life? The authors warn that people become serial success seekers when they don't have a vision. If you don't have a vision yet, how can you expand your awareness to discover your vision?

Achievement can be a drug. How will you come into alignment with your purpose instead?

When people are engaged in what they're working on and have a sense of meaning, they are more likely to be fulfilled in life. Do you feel like you're engaged and have meaning?

How will you work on your purpose daily?

What is you "why"? If you know your why, you will know what moves you forward.

If you don't have direction yet, go ahead and pick a direction anyhow. It's better to focus on something than nothing.

Chapter Fourteen of The One Thing

Is your purpose also your priority in life?

What is your goal for the present?

What type of goals will you set so you can be where you want to be in the future?

Chapter Fifteen of The One Thing

Do you consider yourself to be productive?

To pursue your one thing you should block off your free time, the time required for your one thing, and then your planning time, in this order. The authors' advice is to keep working until you finish the one thing that you have to do today. You should work on your one thing for at least four hours per day. What will your schedule look like now?

| |
| |
| |
| |

Do you ever block off time for vacation or a long weekend? It's a good idea to take vacations so that you have the energy and motivation to pursue your life's work.

| |
| |
| |
| |
| |
| |
| |
| |
| |
| |

Are you more of a maker or more of a manager? Do you create products and write or do you oversee projects?

| |
| |
| |
| |

What are your long term goals? What are your five year goals? When do you usually make plans for the new year? It's best to formulate plans a few month before the new year and not at the last minute.

How often do you review your goals?

How will you create a distraction free environment? What supplies do you need to bring with you?

What do you usually get distracted by? You can use the focusing question to figure out how to get rid of distractions.

Chapter Sixteen of The One Thing

Are you committed to mastering your goal and calling?

Are you getting the results that you want? Will your methods lead you to the results you want? In other words, are they effective?

Do you hold yourself accountable for getting the results you want and doing the work required to get there?

What are you a master of?

Do you complete your work the entrepreneurial way or the purposeful way? The entrepreneurial way is the natural way that people work. The purposeful approach takes some thinking and skills.

What do you do when you reach a ceiling?

Do you take ownership of your outcomes?

Chapter Seventeen of The One Thing

Do you have a hard time saying "no" to things that don't serve you?

How will you deal with the chaos around you when you focus on your one thing for too long? It's normal for other aspects of life to get a bit chaotic when you embrace your one thing.

How will you take care of yourself? It's important to take care of one's health and not sacrifice it.

How do you start of your day and what breakfast do you eat?

How will you energize yourself in the first few hours of your day?

Do you feel that your environment supports you?

Chapter Eighteen of The One Thing

Do you have faith in what you're doing?

What are some of your regrets?

What matters most to you in life?

Thank you for reading and writing!

We hope you learned something new and were able to plan out your major goal.

We care about your reading experience here at Book Nerd and want to provide you with thorough and insightful book guides.

We'd like to give you a virtual high five for reading until the very end. You're a great reader!

Before we part ways, do you mind leaving us a review on Amazon? We would appreciate that greatly, and your support will help us create more book guides in the future.

Thanks again!

Yours Truly,

Book Nerd Team

73073607R00035

Made in the USA
Columbia, SC
02 September 2019